You & I...How Incredible!

Photography copyright © 1997 by Virginia Dixon

Text copyright © 1997 by Garborg's Heart 'n Home, Inc.

Design by Thurber Creative

Published by Garborg's Heart 'n Home, Inc.

P.O. Box 20132, Bloomington, MN 55420

All rights reserved. No part of this book may be reproduced in any form without permission in writing from the publisher.

Scripture quotations marked NIV are taken from the HOLY BIBLE, NEW INTERNATIONAL VERSION® NIV®. Copyright © 1973, 1978, 1984 by International Bible Society. All rights reserved.

Scripture quotations marked TLB are taken from The Living Bible, © 1971. Used by permission of Tyndale House Publishers, Inc., Wheaton, IL 60189. All rights reserved.

You and I... How Incredible!

A loving relationship is a wanting to celebrate, communicate, and know another's heart and soul.

LEO BUSCAGLIA

Looking back on all that we've shared and all that is yet to come, I realize that nothing life may offer me could make me happier than a future filled with loving you.

Love is, above all, the gift of oneself.

JEAN ANOUILH

My lover spoke and said to me, "Arise, my darling, my beautiful one, and come with me. See! The winter is past; the rains are over and gone. Flowers appear on the earth; the season of singing has come, the cooing of doves is heard in our land.... Arise, come, my darling; my beautiful one, come with me."

SONG OF SONGS 2:10-13 NIV

My true-love hath my heart, and I have his,
By just exchange one for another given:
I hold his dear, and mine he cannot miss,
There never was a better bargain driven:
My true-love hath my heart, and I have his.

His heart in me keeps him and me in one,
My heart in him his thoughts and senses guides:
He loves my heart, for once it was his own,
I cherish his because in me it bides:
My true-love hath my heart, and I have his.

Sir Philip Sidney,
"My True-Love Hath My Heart"

There is a camaraderie unique to lovers. It grows out of the unromantic demands of daily living. It is each one given to the other, dividing life's burdens and joys. It is faith in their commitment tightly bound into their faith in the God who creates and holds all things together.

God in His ample love embraces our love
with...a sort of tenderness, and we must
tread the Way to Him hand in hand.

SHELDON VANAUKEN

Something that is stronger and deeper
than any words is found in love.

Love does not consist in gazing at each
other but in looking outward together in
the same direction.

ANTOINE DE SAINT-EXUPÉRY

It is a short word, but it contains all:
it means the body, the soul, the life,
the entire being. We feel it as we feel
the warmth of the blood, we breathe it
as we breathe the air, we carry it
in ourselves as we carry our thoughts.
Nothing more exists for us. It is not a
word; it is an inexpressible state indicated
by four letters.

GUY DE MAUPASSANT

These three remain: faith, hope and love.
But the greatest of these is love.

1 CORINTHIANS 13:13 NIV

How do I love thee?
Let me count the ways.
I love thee to the depth and
breadth and height
My soul can reach,
when feeling out of sight
For the ends of Being
and ideal Grace....
And, if God choose,
I shall but love thee better after death.

ELIZABETH BARRETT BROWNING

Love is a desire of the whole being to be
united to some other being.

SAMUEL T. COLERIDGE

Love... is a deep unity, maintained strengthened by habit; partners ask, and receive, "Being in love" first moved love enables them to keep the that the engine of marriage is run.

by the will and deliberately
reinforced by the grace which both
from God.
them to promise fidelity: this quieter
promise. It is on this love
being in love was the explosion
that started it. C. S. Lewis

Love keeps on growing through life's joys and tears, bringing a fragrance that sweetens with years.

ROY LESSIN

Many waters cannot quench love; rivers cannot wash it away.

SONG OF SOLOMON 8:7 NIV

Love. No greater theme can be emphasized. No stronger message can be proclaimed. No finer song can be sung. No better truth can be imagined.

CHARLES R. SWINDOLL

Whenever I've needed someone to share my joy, or someone to hold me when my world rips to pieces, you're there. And I know you will be — tomorrow, always.

— MAYA V. PATEL

Love is very patient and kind.... If you love someone you will be loyal to him no matter what the cost. You will always believe in him, always expect the best of him, and always stand your ground in defending him.

1 CORINTHIANS 13:4,7,8 TLB

Love is always bestowed as a gift freely,
willingly, and without expectation....
We don't love to be loved, we love to love.

LEO BUSCAGALIA

Love is the Morning and Evening Star.
It is the air and light of every heart, builder
of every home, kindler of every fire on every
hearth. It was the first dream of immortality.
It fills the world with melody.
Love is the magician, the enchanter, that
changes worthless things to joy, and makes
right royal kings of common clay.

ROBERT G. INGERSOLL

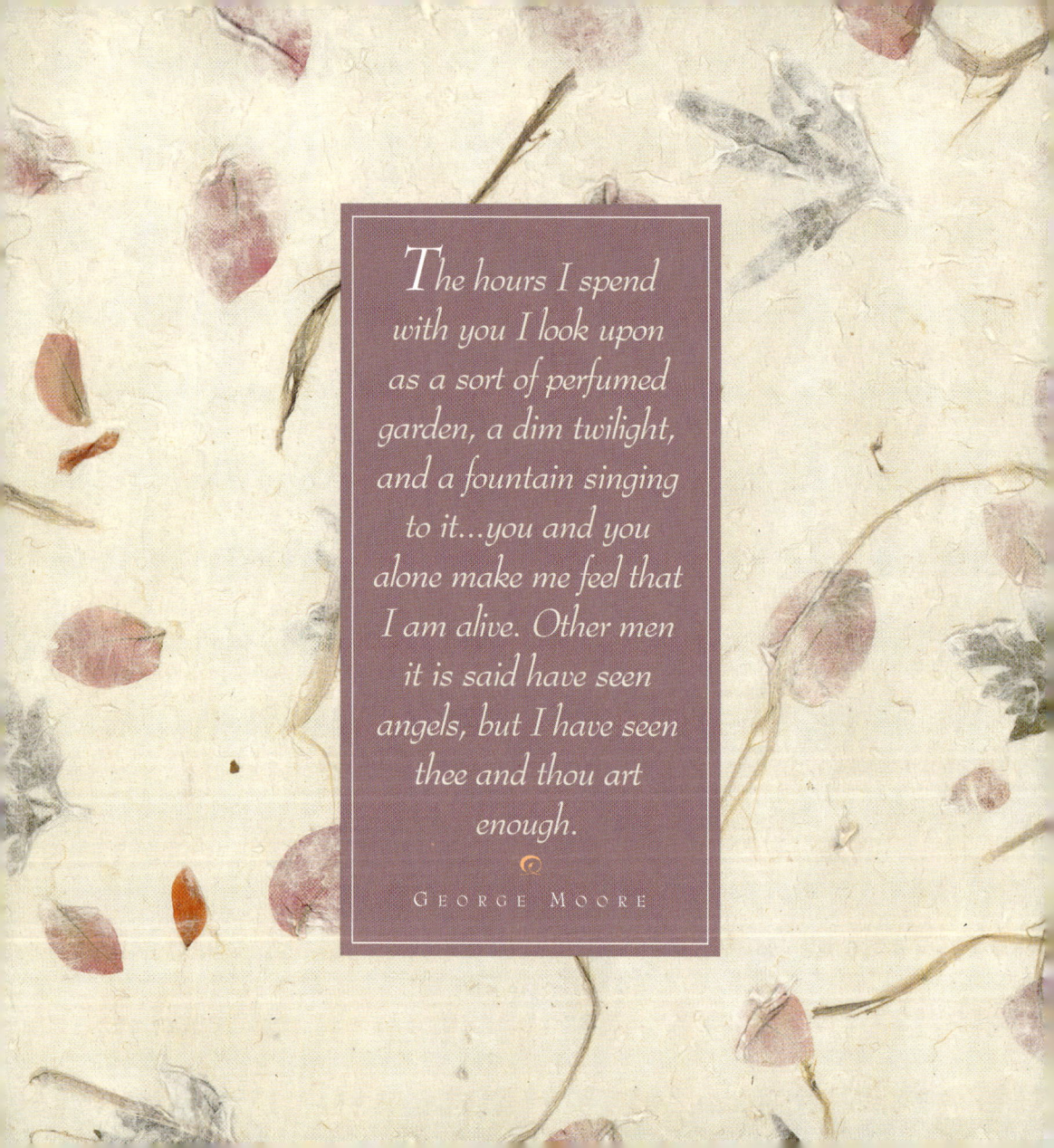

The hours I spend with you I look upon as a sort of perfumed garden, a dim twilight, and a fountain singing to it...you and you alone make me feel that I am alive. Other men it is said have seen angels, but I have seen thee and thou art enough.

GEORGE MOORE

Is the key to love in
All three—along with moonlight,
gettings and
and room rent, pearls of memory
Lock not away

passion, knowledge, affection?
roses, groceries, givings and forgivings,
forgettings, keepsakes
along with ham and eggs....
your love nor keep it hid.   CARL SANDBURG

Love seems the swiftest, but it is the slowest of all growths. No man or woman really knows what perfect love is until they have been married a quarter of a century.

MARK TWAIN

Love makes burdens lighter, because you divide them. It makes joys more intense, because you share them. It makes you stronger, so that you can reach out and become involved with life in ways you dared not risk alone.

You are always new. The last of
your kisses was ever the sweetest;
the last smile the brightest; the
last movement the gracefullest.

JOHN KEATS

May the Lord make your love
increase and overflow for
each other.

1 THESSALONIANS 3:12 NIV

I love thee with the breath,
smiles, tears of all my life!

ELIZABETH BARRETT BROWNING